DOUBLE ZERO

DOUBLE ZERO

CHRIS HOSEA

PRELUDE

The Prelude Press LLC
PO Box 110593
Brooklyn, NY 11211

Stu Watson and Robert C.L. Crawford, Publishers

Designed by Mike Newton

preludebooks.com
preludemag.com

Library of Congress Cataloging-in-Publication Data has been applied for.

ISBN 978-0-9907030-7-5

for Lillian

*Don't seek that all that comes about should come about as you wish,
but wish that everything that comes about should come about
just as it does, and then you'll have a calm and happy life.*

—Epictetus

CONTENTS

I Love You 1

Player Zero 3

Who Is the Big Winner 5

This Is Going to Be the Year You Can Feel It 7

Parted on the Side 9

Good Conduct Well Chastised 13

In the Shit 15

How to Fall Out of Love 17

Take Cover Before Striking 18

Walking to Birmingham 19

Paper Dolls 20

Richmond, London 22

Fresh Stubble Air 23

Real Raspberries 26

The Final Countdown 28

Dead a Long Time 32

Little Black Book 33

Little Blue Book 34

Little Yellow Book 35

Little Silver Book 36

Little Salt Book 37

Little Carbon Book 39

Purple Vinyl 40

Molly Ringwald 42

White on White 43

Catch Play 45

Same Time 46

Hurt the Stream 47

Nothing to Watch but the Road 48

American Terrorist 50

This Is for You 51

Professor Marvel 52

Thursday I Forget Her Name 53

Homegrown Cell 54

Tape Hiss 55

Wild Bunny Pie 57

Know Your Name 59

We May Be Free 61

So Many Fortresses 63

DOUBLE ZERO

I LOVE YOU

if kindness and morals hold the lead
I'd like to push my head up your soul
if I could trail a fuzzy cloud-like box kite
maybe they'd see bright parcels thrum
surrounded by abstract thing violence
nothing but nuggets can I draw today
rocking rocking car gone out of
you go come forward harder
tearful men pillow your memory
I too believe you saved me by the way
you say one thing and do another
how you wash the thing that washes
perfectly applied bright red lipstick
because I didn't think I could shape
out of green bulbs blue pink envelopes
I like it in here away from prying eyes
from being told to play the hits
think if you slip your hand down
my vector which is aimed at you
to think yesterday I forwarded you a copy
to slip on out for a few months golden
color of the fire we are to feed upon
and with inserts redolent of lavender
to wake and split the difference
your Aztec face open like a melon
that watches small ink marks cross to ruin
with little habits sudden italics
anything good to look at seems suspect
and no one keeps anyone's council
you opened a hole in my lifetime
I fall without a sound into night sky
to pose like metal thinker replica
I will keep more copies promises
torsos striking gently after ice cream plug

I miss being bruised not recommended
existing as beauty with sharp invisible edge
mercurial long indented nose above flat lip
in eye of a spiritual champion
who peers in mirror in showroom
at you bent frontwards as on crusade
I could scout better technical terms
even and dry as powder put on popcorn
sudden freedom of unlimited snapshots
young squabbling moralists in cutoffs
divided into the blessed and the bored
if I could daily quit more new normal events
as how you throw beauty in faces
sinister sun to welcome kindle your burn
never before on video easy scoff your shining hair
a ship and a pony and a ruled page there
I opened a hole in my lifetime
let everyone be seen prettier
so relaxed listening whole time calm
to lose myself in decades unnoticed
under long thin blue bulbs in hallways
and what about blowouts self to self
the most private joke same author
same reader shake all else off with effort
the wrecked plane underground wires all rust
having hit the candle dimmed the lamp
surveilled by family friends bosses moles
sucking simple syrup up colored straws
if there is a good time that is good
for you and me and billions of others right now
this instant slightly dazed as storms gather
wanting only a notion vigorously true
some total complete agreement to destroy
your name and my name forever

PLAYER ZERO

these tough as rot
flowering tabloids today I get myself
to be gone now nothing hurting nothing
but more to say zip too of when
I lifted hat labeled beef brand
cap poisoned blood it flew
over through urns and curves noted
not discussed when after hot
fritters look at me she said see my past
like rose rose on thorny stem that ass
these torn portions see my spirituality
full face as to develop old older
halt paltry wisdom exchange satisfactory
rations inexact rational planes fold
and then was she flew up against dropped pilot
to plead wanted medium term resin plot
to a tilt sniff quite yuck her quaint
it sticks in you shed fallen bills bits
kindling you gather in view of park golden
yes goods grandfather may sketch
sunup first thing wetter woozy
at these my magic hands trim wick
open unfurl your sail billowy
at her as good late picture melody
those days not a dry window in the
yet curtains draw such as her apply
at yo-yo bulge chords herded quietly
as wrap me rumination bag fat and sour
drop these white American pounds
my contraption up and over past moons
say afterlife pastel castle sigh sigh
spoilers fall there so few was it lust
chivalry undead learned shorthand late
her shoulder buzz cuts afternoons

hello not to comet you back
string me cord-whip me Eureka me hose me
down studio boy you are good prone
blotter up on the in-breath
foreign plunder tamps soil
all there so and so prayer zippers
work together type to her lips
two spaces sound the old real bell
get back in your corner be ashamed man boy
nipple head shut hard not tomorrow's tip
get on up about a spout of water
how stiffly your appetite thrums dumb
your harm would wipe liquid crystal you
would hide in your smartphone such love

WHO IS THE BIG WINNER

Grinning, tallish, gangly, elbows akimbo
and playful, she slaps me hard, I get it
flash backwards, when we first met at MoMA
very brief reference to a few clipped, I mean
confused, plans for oil paintings to live off
demolitions in homage to a cartoon ghost
grinning, tallish, gangly, elbows akimbo
you can't have it all, but you can have some
of everything, a fuck, a smoke, a random new
something I love about as much as getting employee
of the month at Target, she whiffs of sweet
back Brooklyn someday afternoon, finally making it
in a big way, commissions and credits and captions
she got up on my knee, got off on my thigh, I mean
confused like any artist hopes to live off her art
grinning, tallish, gangly, elbows akimbo
eventually her dreams come true, excited I mean
she chokes on me, doesn't stop, hopes to be busy
literally always, time flies back, I have gone from
mostly deep breaths to consume four bananas fast
dancing at Glasslands and Home Sweet Home
and that's freedom, man, freedom, the freedom of
grinning, tallish, gangly, elbows akimbo
I feel confused feelings but also so turned on
maybe it's love, I want more, she's afraid
not to veg out on some faraway beach you know
I've been looking through old snapshots, my closet
apartment on seventh and B, nineteen ninety-nine
my old flame green apple cream in snap flash lip slack
old days, anyone who ever lived them will agree, hurt spread
like fertilizer, if you have time to look, redolent in late faces, I
used to think if this ever happened, not that it would, but
would I turn myself over to a program, witness and teach
the prematurely aged, never to be seen again

but no, I can't do that yet, what turns me on right now
are things and people and places and people
who are free and busy not free and easy
grinning, tallish, gangly, elbows akimbo
I mean confused, yeah, but also so turned on
I didn't think she should run from desire I told her so
she smacked out dizzy-making selfies sweet verbs
in her way optimistic as an artist's statement read over and again
optimistic yes she acts crazy in relationships so she says
the sex is hot and playful she slaps me hard makes pink marks
just hard in the face her stare a glint in a mess of acne under lank
brown hair a kind of situation summons like it's so hard
so crazy it just might work her tits so they spurt milk
I mean it's happened I am confused but also so turned on
maybe it's love, it is love, I want more, she's afraid

THIS IS GOING TO BE THE YEAR YOU CAN FEEL IT

This is the thing it has to be
curls of wind on the inside
to be a wife tensed ready
for the attacker who just like
quit avoiding silent steps
the sun fell like a coin into a large glass
of soda of who else could stir class
without ever stopping being
hot what got me opens the ducts
lovely intimate ass candy a sweep
who could sing too I never did her
rudely the camera pulled deep inside
that there pocket snuggle for long so
long you say I have arrived a green
leaf only pressed only to hot oily glass
I just threw up in my couch
you trembled with me then and tomorrow
America stacked plastic tabs to see
who would pay green garage door
opener of a kind absolute beauty
don't stop jones for universal health
gay nuptials I'd rather not be misunderstood
in a meadow or suburban field
but in the midst of your bachelorette
I know no function rapid drought streaming
in all your digital devices churning rivers
flopping salmon flick the sound off sound on
heat pipes meet a metal crotch her hand wetter than
a sponge wedged in a U-pipe
its style so mysterious you think annual report
rooms and electronics heaters refrigerators vibrators
I don't want you anymore
I want fourteen personal days
and that singer's buttocks like

his lips hardly barely moving
and a message comes from across the sea
when I check my email again it
gets into places you were friends let it go
you got thinking you could key poems to virals
built a ship from specie strictly a kind of guide
stars look to move so silent flaming gases
a hand shot out from a blouse cuff
to brush my special fly my oh my
sacred skin it is silk pillows these nubby conduits
could put my name in granite someday soon
all pressure invisible stabbing to winter's spleen
flopping but stuck fast and be breathing
the wind tosses the rain and the rain pushes the wind
don't fuck so close to me I know that story
following a exemplary throw the profile of a creeper you
I have a word for you I gain weight talking
lifting pants without hands a pretty lament for you
yes you do not know this is for you yet it is
on the tip of my tongue in you this is your ear

PARTED ON THE SIDE

Oh my God this girl fingers at knob
when I left my home and my family
I was only sixteen I left my home
and my family moved to Baltimore
I had never shaved a virgin
pale as a ghost hair so brown
looked black I thought the doors
of sex would open up and take me
I boxed my Henry Miller paperbacks
my compact discs and cassettes
this girl my God how she stood
still she was moving in every molecule
there was a flood of sunlight a great fire
in the vestibule she fast at the little wheel
I was going to live in her same building
on North Charles the McCoy
face every day the long lawn they called
the beach that grandiose entryway
to Johns Hopkins to college
all was new I had never seen
an ass that round or high ride so full
her thin figure moving not moving
like a candle flame in windless chamber
a cousin put that song on a tape
I got it in the mail I didn't like to admit
it was so good when it came on
another boy gave me Pink Flag
part of Chairs Missing on a Maxell XL 90
and I was the fly the outdoor miner
as tall as her looking at her on one knee
face at the wall of glass slots
she could have been a boy
her hair the color of hardwood floor
parted flat tamped down with wet comb

this was 1990 but no mousse no iron for her
in vestibule sunset my God this girl
her huge men's T-shirt white as white
no logo no slogan it hung loose about
her pipe-like rubbery mechanical
shoulders flesh color of strong coffee
that all the cream in the world has been
poured into yet you see so faint
a tincture tawny when she turned around
blurted out I can't do this
I looked at her then the first time
opened her mailbox surprised she
didn't know combination locks
was it flirting tapes in the mail to boys or girls
you wanted to show them how
with an arc not so much planned flirting
as fallen down upon so they could feel
thrill of chance snow wet pocket
getting stiff nipples or a hard cock
you could send an email but there
was no video online no music
you had to alter a plastic thing
all we had compact discs and records
radios and mix tapes to give
I couldn't really talk to her even
hours in her room on North Charles
in McCoy Hall drinking her
talking I don't know why I thought
I should put myself down every time
I said I was a bad lover an idiot
I mean it was true I was sixteen
I knew I loved her so it had to be
I was bottom dog couldn't win
she told me at home in Rio

boys and girls only friends fooled
around to see how it was touch and kiss
we were alone I freaked when she said
looked at my hands held my back firm
said nothing went back to my room
in those days North Charles was fine but
liquor stores on St Paul were cased in bulletproof
I met two boys who grew weed on Calvert
their row house greenhouse beside a crack door
I didn't like to go as far as Guilford late
Hippy Andy lost half his left hand trying to
block blast of sawed-off twelve-gauge
he called it his flipper laughed I brought
weed sometimes mushrooms from Abell
back to her but that wasn't really her thing
the fire in her burning like sage
always same every time played
but different her time that time was hers
in time she was a dancer eyes greeny
a dancer even sitting in lecture
standing half aloof with a Parliament
when human traffic moved down the beach
always it seemed there was a floor to go to
I liked to talk to see if she would go with me
with my words hold them at a certain distance
waltzing like at middle school cotillion space
between us for the Holy Spirit I'd get high
listen to her the sound of her breath
I loved to hear and my friend Beezup said
as he handed me a long glass bong in his penthouse
at the Hopkins House we could see the harbor
alight and he laughed and said you're too hard
on yourself go have fun with a lot of girls
don't get so serious but I said look at you you

just lost Catherine to Evan Dando from the
Lemonheads but she'll be back he said
she shaved her pussy when he pressed her
said he had to shave too it itched like hell for days
and the Lemonheads came and Dando charmed her
weeks later Catherine returned and Beezup took her back
she said they made it to Phoenix after night on bus
when all the lights went out in McCoy
except for exit signs and mounted floods
kids were drinking National Bohemian and running
around with candles flashlights and lighters
and suddenly I was face to face with her in dim stairwell
her eyes opened up I started falling like a moon forever
she gave me a hug I could feel her
pelvic bone her small unripe breasts brush
in distance joking screams laughter
she saw through me tilted her chin
looped a finger through my belt
all my hairs at attention God I almost died
too long I stood and never moved to kiss her
when I went I went to Cambridge in September
I mailed her mix tape after mix tape
The Velvets Run Run Run
Tom Petty Don't Back Down Blondie's
Hanging on the Telephone Lemonheads Mallo Cup
and Waterfall by the Stone Roses Happy Mondays
Step On Man Called Sun by Verve De La Soul's
Eye Know Bob Dylan It's All Over Now Baby Blue
I had a few snapshots of a lot of half-thoughts
bits of memories precious fictions losing definition
each tape a shrine to her way of always dancing
voyages toward the miraculous I wanted to ship me
lanterns hung on the caboose as it pulls off for good

GOOD CONDUCT WELL CHASTISED

I feel freedom subway in my head
so silent touching everything Sunday I can
wake up not go at large pretty spaces
a tunnel you have where I could dig my spade
bury my skull ultimately last looks
religions valid as any other a certain irony
like yours swinging thin bleached braid
around trash look Goth-black AWOL
prep school guise shows off your ink well
against the silken gash of history or so said
a sticker over your head when you locked
on me slammed your butt against door
too many strangers would try to pry in
and your dead-eyed stare got stuck
I made you look in mirror for self-reflexivity
you had it in teeth a fave stick stuck
my too-cold pinky wet into your jaw
when your mouth took in each day's power
figures in memory stood on steps vague
with hammer grim aspect mustache violet
water glue gilds us customers as useless
sugar pills broken friendship bracelet ripped
pieces in purse a purse not ever a bag
thank God drop your hand on key bunch
too soon so much tiny crystals ants around
native to your room we live and study among them
potential learnings potent sexual seminars
best practices how to cheat at Boggle
you will own this town singing hoarsely
though fucking scared from steeple so scared
above City Hall singing I am available
I am a flesh bell went to market jingling
don't give a damn who knows it
sweater hand coarse worn damp never warmer

smooth reasons you'd use to graduate once more
and again drop out sometime so long ago to sleep
I never knew him and it's cheap but you have
to bargain because to bargain is the custom
or be rude I brought myself alone to go down up
to swirling surface close as I could huff of
transdermal toxins be alone like piston
solar panel middle-aged bachelor padding
your hall can you plug me into your grid
beautiful separate girl looked at first for form alone
why didn't I take a picture would it have lasted
longer thighs straighter pale pickets white tubes
true I've got scorn want you come back hit me
air is best energy drink come empty buses come candles
bonfires end rent party come asphalt summer soon

IN THE SHIT

down in the arrested
ricochet the meeting was
what they called the place no
one went to pay and use
pay and use upper arm
screen flashing the approach she
completed the form copied it
you can see the stiff
paper buckle talk tock
talk tock talk tock I will
say to you for example it is hard
for me what you see
you went through not that I would
ever even pretend like she
understands the way a girl in heat
is hot at the moment said leave me
here I am not alone here I want
to be the only one not yours
in the kitchen stopping the talk
of carbon credits patriarchy raster dots
tattoos they grope stretch wrinkle
into the open fridge glow
under the reggae I was crying a man
fast forward locked in a relationship
kids and everything from starter
to free-range midway I sobbed
for a canvasser for corporate wind
put a mint in her if I could I
heard a youth in anger call her father creepy
and I could sense non-vegan licking
coming in my throat hurling after eating caps
after pastrami and pizza and a Slim Jim
to shake off at thirty cold iron ballpoint bullshit
elope with one green vending machine ring

pause the video so you see it flicker on her friend
as in what we now are doing special moment
I could tell you stories lacking
any interest at all least of all
for me I am a professional breathing mouth
rates bitten sound to snuff the prick
of some man's angry art
lacking good ape imitations
rookie plastic bit broken tiny slug
will have to matter it is curfew we wear
out conference call tomorrow don't you hate
saying we because be honest who among us
hasn't tried on eyeliner
sucked some cock online written tougher
bumper stickers for all to see
from a gently speeding train to see not
quite what I mean an analog selfie
why was that beautiful girl sobbing
at a black plastic box circa 1994
within a line of karaoke Journey
she was the crème creamy sinner at heart
and would have told the intruder what Wreck did
that we would kill him we or one of our men
look loaded famous chin up kiddo
she actually pushed my chin with her palm
and we got to get away I got to go forward
get back to Mom's house got to put down
tracks get fed pay out some slack death's head

HOW TO FALL OUT OF LOVE

Feet first summer gristle on bone
speak nothing of yourself to you
her golden leg hair makes sun sob and stands
to point out now food value of a squirrel
to approach a microphone and pull
down be tame in a spot-lit pen scream
nobody gets up to leave heavy belly
or carry damages made plainer
distributing listeners differently now
us and the room cut off from sunlight
when an angry joke bakes into metaphor
painted table fruits are set back
a murmur suggesting your own faces
famous paintings photographs
never to be parted from historical record
the daylight would command patience
the owner's manual for this register
would have you lathered shaved
as with wild boar pâté as with roadside
concession just open your briefcase after
minutes of words at a spill for it is far
later sooner the bar will close us out
into streets amid landmarks hidden
in a sky blacker that is closer now
than thought

TAKE COVER BEFORE STRIKING

versions of women girls easy then off some swing free
an empty park I have tight press being jogging asides
gently freaking out just a little too hard wrist back teary
do artists who die young know how I'm sorry often but not
really at task you get stuck near corners paintbrushes can't
touch every gear shaft a lingam condensation into wind
hey wait everybody it's a remark we really wanted a drop
until you break boom and burn I'd like an acting job
now to be paid big among nerds rock stars adrift
putting tables into rooms to new use polish new barricades
said of a man he could walk by we would never know he bleeds
all in his mouth steady blood pour duly swallowing
see smart jackets spray air filaments dust dander glitter rests
will I look bad in your year-end rearview now I know we are
too free or not half there to work it out all but drape myself
over your near edge empty pool leaves scratch at blue gut
you know without articulating cigarettes shy of true love
given the mouth of a stranger that hasn't been dabbed a child
given a commuter's twitching thigh naked JPEGs I lost on purpose
to be killed of a sudden it's not the middle it's some collapsing line
part of the third act you expect praise from boss mother Jack
a salute from a pal's cool dad why not make another kid renew
effusions vaguely celebratory a great-aunt's panic attack prank
check in mister rest because tonight you must dance like before
then you go open look around you can call me gentler
keep notes glasses filmed on tray bum knee you would never
sit down only just come in ID glow kittens the weathered neighbor
then such dark as citronella candles we guess won't drink flame
you have done well for yourself this lovely home hospitality
you have time for little things such as matter more than
whoever on electric guitar like ripped satin in hood fan
have you tried anal I ask and make the air quotes with my eyes
reality is a star in her heart lights up if you can see it only

WALKING TO BIRMINGHAM

On the towpath to eternal life I just can't
genially gesture at assumed outlines
imagined as having been left alone to bend
and surface saying really something in the air
petty as grievances swept I soon remembered
never again would votes be tallied by hand
customer service be king at this hotel
I made my hand to ape the shadow of a gun
a mechanical bull so unlike any real
steer afraid of sun glare cowers half-hidden
in hollows sounding sometime nostrils
horns from lungs large luggage be fashioned
preserved unknown you not listening how
anyway to word solo deep down the well
feathers taste when you suck at torn jacket
sleeve faint marks where phone rode brick
late months buy this poetry American life
everyone extra familiar too thirsts for stiff rope
sex scandal revenge Finland summer coast forsworn
so pure sex steps take less still less they startle
no more buzz lips tickle knees forever fevered
is it the house trees the large view beyond
persons famous he casts as he who shuns love
I took on more causes to refute serial habits
being outside I struck to sleep a tower's mossy butt
big trees between towpath and canal no more barges
worn yellow gravel path soft sponge runs in sock
it was the world and not me it was the world
that moved arrow fast blown turning its cold seam
it was the world surface slick diffusing starlight
and not me wrapped in warm perpetual fall
low great heavy cotton ball stone-colored clouds
it was the world it was the world it is there
I walk with twilight on and on far roll on marble on
sky murk on low clouds on legs clap past on ways

PAPER DOLLS

test what buried spark she drove to
groove in what connects an art graven form
all dropped made them heavy felt in there hurt
dead rabbits use inside voices softener city
line let out vector tremble dips from stick
dead lake ham sandwich accident
sinks so fast soggy feeling to squishy mulch
plumb line can you swim you belly bottom
then American green fabric travel nude feet
trace a toe sharpied flower permanent hangs out
symbol for to hover taken spaces stone brace corners
fast at times though wind goes under gets to lift
and below try breathing loam classes support
so you could hear yourself think you think this is
colors day one alarms to empty amber
were you there when I called you were are
now or never floors slant above at left
down as them windows smack shut sills kiss
with a suck girl trembles dayrooms she is
more pretty becoming empty just what goes on
bachelor father feeling to plug your butt I mean my own
sleep-robed synthetic vibrations good
put out her page-boy at fast highway miles
clowning star-stuck pair of eyes hungering
lurch at the light to crane the wrong way
a primitive paste bright light slap me it's the hurt I like
and though the forest do darken I don't stir
you are a desirable person kind and patient
I found a grey sock and some underwear looked like
you are a narcissistic person who cares little for others
turn it over tie it slide it under places
turn the freshly framed picture to the wall
nimble fingers barely move in spit in drool
you are a successful artist a worthy addition

to our avant-garde tradition
you can disassociate what you to do pay for
she is Christmas a fresh tree just screwed at base
you are a good friend a loyal person
you are generous with friends and strangers
you lack empathy and show disregard for others' feelings
you misrepresent your emotional needs
this comes out of my head drips down it and more
the work is never the world never your energy too
why do you have to listen to where that could get
thank you for making this possible it means a lot
like teaching me about art
and how to make a living around it a split life
in which you cordon off a half and disappear

RICHMOND, LONDON

guts first offence in a twist her fault slips
away down elevator stairs I take double
so as to keep a sense how chilly May
days wet stuffed toys sad fun on stoops
can I plan to be in my way with you
elevator door gone backwards onto Fir plaza
me still like a whistle teachers cops kettle
ignore pants around shoes spray then shower
she had a briefcase crocodile accessories
I hadn't eaten meat in days indoors toed a tub
of margarine full old washers and slugs sick
of it couldn't catch your gaze with my iPhone
and you even more gloomy steady state
if I could always spy your thigh your eye
when you kill a butt against a sill lady of mists
you are a cipher to me whistling no account
I see a family full of invalids sweetbreads
you worry me the way you worry you're too
ready to end lives if it comes to that you
know who would kill for you and do it too

FRESH STUBBLE AIR

for Bettina Marx

i. face a

frame though it go from sight
above behind around afar
elements now slow or climates
fast but if rain could purple
scurrying damage so stain could linger
as running tap smells of birch leaves
der Wasserhahn rinnt its line dripping
in domestic play destiny is destiny
pink rare as if cut steak smeared
down wall down to your heel level
lines as in floorboards or louvers and stays
intervals establish space high then split it
out of fear of loss of fear being close-knit pride
hits again it should have been made mad
to give gifted pupils thin bannisters to handle
tender striplings in grim cottage pluck elbow skin
for the makers who know to stop clock palms
staying indoors smoking freely is cut from past
and you see cream canvas furniture
recline toward violent waves set sail to capsize
a red caboose shoots off panting wet
paintings clamped in place like lumber
hooked to water flown out of earshot
pressure travel trailing ripples
this future mainstream future can't not know
chair legs must be termed anew let us call them
mold cheese marinade sills askew
clean enough lost honeybees
in districts found seeping sap
anatomy charts printed pixelated
dinner tied tight wrapped in oilcloth
pictures tack mirror scratched

yesterday carries no balance debt service
ahead awoke yet halts under lintels
one walks limp another today direction
find stains darken bleaches whiten
pool colonies marked for pollution
mossy accident handkerchief stiff
in pocket last opened 19th century
said great coat was round shady bird
bath a look we hardly ever leave
off within house inertia rushes rushes
this standing race so stop so stop the box
turtle retracts a faceted face

ii. face b

in your corner damp it is in you
sponge your left eye bloods a bit
why we are here account prosaic
few lines notes forgotten on platforms
to be done with art and dry goods are stored
for later sale a spastic master struts fresh
for play at mariners far off mother's hair
folded never more bombed so cold war swell
I fall from on high to smack inky pools
puddle me up live refuse glows to a boil
I am one stitched surface hit hard
unhurt tracers seamed night sky
my mind it would seem to go burst
brained against false door hung
indoors vapors float up in thin mist
this vessel buffeted contains hole
straight at you flesh face cards red
small warm-blooded hurting in a pen
makes me want permission to cross snug
into you is it your area for a first-time domestic

I carry a heavy harpoon laser pointer
to where you haven't lately been
pictures slide off the spatula
and grey-lit bone-light makes wash
traffic shut out on copper corner cornice
night is cavernous restaurant is her hands
bring me without touch suspect memory
I insist on the phrase "from the past"
a mental farewell common-run salute
an archaic predatory type
a harsh attack on dancing plumbing
a threshold of a cheap little house
a flourish they that went by they could hear
his hair gleaming with fragrant oils
his belly bare it seemed to wink
at a place you always must go
to humble your mouth at seams of crotch
to wake alone and light does
nothing ghostly furniture hardware
tells you you are not a mirror not never
below light curved water air

REAL RASPBERRIES

edge of known stinger stuck
to not in fresh white meat dent
must have been cooked fried
better grilled girl then maps bottom
shelf see women damp their sauce
species in that histories well down
are petrified cushions for thing gathering
yes aware of that album video game
bombs under Berlin your bedroom you
an age in years he beside a lack
lacking papers highway pink pants
they said so travel office posters no
one went to take black Santa
black that's never funny that
I'm such a kind of rake half a year
downstate saying I want games
raspberry splotch on down white jeans
as if she can always taste
the period jam style hers in which
still wearing them real raspberry
independent instructional films
shot through with what looked like
honey money I know
you know about my soul I told you
you would your brain on same bra
most prized device giving me shivers
briny inedible salad heavy metal sprinkles
personally I'm always a tad surprised
when there's nothing there not aghast
but what is going room olive space oil
it runs on after the fold in
her corner back up mouthguard
plastic or metal container a coach the
old salt never hard your friends said

I could torture him draw it outside
so it could get very real facebook
Hermès messenger dental dam
who else is a pen pusher for the transcript
with a warm side of hand but no go fuck yourself
this time we run it tougher speed of blab
on the vocals Mercedes-Benz bag mouth
you can take a go fuck yourself
from every pause longer than a minute
an alien after all will always irreducibly
let it be as hated Beatles how'd they
get my pills ready so fast
all nines so and forth but and wait
above a whisper step forward
not in real life just a little video game
you stack the bodies you see when you
discover they are aliens lying caring
you just char them
with the flamethrower there are more
if they are aliens there's nothing
for it kill with fire some aliens will leave
of their own accord but they always come
back so just torch them up right that laugh
they are all the same in the end
they are all stacked saves on digging
better that way forget clips chips coins
dead packs pricks it's legal just
torch stack more will come give a warm
damn there are people watching you
you can see them or at least imagine them
up on stage their little future eyes

THE FINAL COUNTDOWN

It was behind that
frozen dispersing scene the last
in her gut she knew
light curved laughter it was light
compared to sins
head on they were too
distressing to habit
supposedly puncture-proof
and misunderstood the majority
perhaps were believers themselves
their scorn for nerds
the only true way
to avoid recurrent headaches
back into hatches with luggage
your delicate language of limbs
pretending sleep while
mooning at the moon and I drove
roads at least wouldn't run out nor woods
before the countdown piped up
in tones of an anthem
easier to sing and older than the real
the weather stopped happening
anymore anymore or more
became an unchanging alarm
to say there were cars and thus people
all atmospheres closed like the lips
a horror quilt stitched
for a precious museum
its staff so obsessed with wall texts
I put in time myself
for being invisible to my own thoughts
unlocking a gate in a well that led to stars
making myself dark hard and mean
turning off the cell phone

for good that time
that moment in prisoner when
you decide if they will ever find you
knowing you can't
avoid being part of the plot
either way some filigree
on a frame cracking
a smile to break up lineage
confuse words of generosity
with words of aggression
buying up misunderstood spaces
of cleverness and love
the clever spicing the love
so that inside the reader a beloved place
hurts the heart is sprained
and worse considered a mere machine
responsive to blunt attacks hurtful words
cartoon lovers don moon boots
and the lip of space
is brought curbside
we are of it and in it already
for good and more perhaps for worse
hurtling ourselves
at targets we implode
such that the simple time taken
to read a text message
requires you build
Wonder Woman's plane
or diorama hairless girl and all
in your arms the liquid scent of sex
is an acid destroying systems
these repeated attacks
may worsen the conditions
so we grow to hate each

other and ourselves
well imagine it is the two of us
fucking reader
jealous of the short half
hour of fucking
joining our parts
hiding revolutions in each other
to do good or hurt less
I slide under you and lick your asshole
because I love your asshole
that is a fact at least
g force spins a fresh globe
out of this one we roll
as if suspended airless
on and under fingers
in my or your hair brains
blending just humming energies
each time and then again
our natural disinclination to
fuck me
the good excuses
little deceptions
make vacuums bloom
fishtails scatter time
make it drizzle from our parts again
all down the floor the bedclothes
so we don't know much
longer who we are
we are locked in it
kicked out into the ether
kissing just from repetition
exploding corpses in the sun
get under me and come
again spring comes

hurting the small flowers
rashes and smells
the old manure
that reminds you of nature's business
even rocks sweating
iron as much a part of
and something someone is sucking
you on the Internet
and I'm licking your other teat
those automated words aim
both inflate and pop a bag
filled with gases hasten us
make our voices tiny precious
scary vicious how
you can say anything
when you've sucked a balloon
the smallest put down now so cute
it is acceptable for you to be
thinking of him while you take me faster
what joins us stretching giving
who doesn't because there isn't just one
of him or one of me or you
in this many universes
or one pussy one cock
so many millions
inhaling exhaling there is less air now it is
become a grip

DEAD A LONG TIME

Those flower pistils shoot photons hottie so so
don't is that dust drugs corners lips yours move
me laminated maps stand half out the dirt
together we commented on it already as if living
our last hours in some crypt fallen down all over
roads to bright conversation tarps festive hangars
talks where I had to point it out to you again
it was collapse it that our heads fishtailed at
to make you care for my long hard my wish
romantic in all things pathetic sore worn palm
yours as a mother on kid's nape makes one go on
possibly in the same town to know you will lie
you find in time the principle of the purse an alert
just atoms never have to decide the gestures seen
from loitering boys probably in the same town
because care is not for you but hurt harder snap
the clasp then you get a sharp look in the theater feel
that two-year-old condom that free religious coin
grey dawning on you in at least one thousand colors
it is morning I am near learn from your phone
a name like rat bastard curry evil Billy Burns
they of precious memory record store cashiers
whiter than their tube sock above knee
they come up and help me remember 1973
putting it in and out of memory boxes for them
bruises that put us on notice of alleys blocked off
so will you roll up in a rug with me pull the ski masks
down we are falling we fall without one sound

LITTLE BLACK BOOK

Gladness is taken away
Therefore I will bewail
Now when they for all that
In the world
Lust of the eyes
Captains of the chariots
Man that doth meditate
Will die here put it
On his head desirable young men
Will put my words in his
Mouth I have caused my terror
Set fire upon her towers
Head like purple will
The unicorn be willing
To serve thee or abide by thy crib
Stoned with stones
The same day
An innumerable multitude
Wicked inventions
I will make
Slew in the city
Refuse and rebel a pure heart
Openeth the ears of men
A band of men I cannot lift up
Take the arrows
He did part them I dreamed
A dream by night
Black horses
Thc bay went forth
Angel that talked
With her suburbs silver
Spread into plates
Asses feeding
He lifted up his eyes and looked
And I from twenty years old
Suffer it to be so now

LITTLE BLUE BOOK

Death of azure and delicate storm
I shall no longer enter to write about
Instruments too full of pride
Were I a painter
With a beautiful advertisement for heaven or hell
I am however willing
I have talked myself into believing that time
I was tan when everyone sang
A baleful perch for parrots and crows
As fast as you can pull the trigger into the crowd
I have no buttons on my vest
From a clever mixture of little lies and rare flowers
This summer the roses are blue
We are therefore obliged
That we be the masters of ourselves, the masters of women
Because man is above all the plaything of his memory
Let's say to wait for myself in China
Respect your parents
The sultan signs idly
For her to be stripped
We are going to find
I take a certain degree of pleasure
In condemning each step that I take is a dream
With mystery in a Venetian mirror
An extremely emotional state
Around fifteen years' old
The first white paper in this dizzying race
To the concentration of your mind
Travel, which is so conducive to shaping
Provided that they guide us
Free of any charming liberty
We believe we are thinking
The genius that watches
In the guise of sorcerers to touch I am
The last person in the world to know

LITTLE YELLOW BOOK

Let's recall independent of her magic
A series of remarks confided by a mature eye
I don't believe at all
What is this good for The Poet—to return to
Music's presence and nothing more
Attributed to Baudelaire
A question closely bound up
To end at penetrating, enveloping, definitive London
As an unconscious hymn on the day
Which lies in shadowy beings who clam up
Always without excuses I'm on stage
I think I can break down on this spring
A hundred years or more from now
Unless there is a genius saying Dance
Certain crystalline airs brief and young
From her bursts out not without grace some
Author hitting it big according to me
Which blazes with charm
With the autumn wind, a rumor
Quickly to hold up a form of beauty turned inside
You just tear off a blank white page
The public Domain we spoke about
The glow of false electric skies
Between the sheets there reigns a silence still

LITTLE SILVER BOOK

Tomorrow will go underground
As an ironing board
Toward other regions more verbal
It was not just the vogue
For a neutral country
Back then in America
I put a hand painted by a sign
I came back a long time
Since the wind tore it up
A virtue for rich people
I really like this kind of game
It was precision optics in short
Before being a motor which transmits her
Cinematic blossoming of virgin
He had enormous weight
Fresh meaning smart
Only so I could make a pun
It had been broken
But that wasn't what kept me
We had to start all over
As a souvenir from Paris
You couldn't control it
Scratch away the rest
Houses which were new at that time
Free and easy
I was considered an artist
I projected each shadow
Which I traced by hand

LITTLE SALT BOOK

I knew to go to Dr. Fu Manchu
Whose goal is the vanishing point
He feels about it in his own breast
And yet the zeal to reform
Taking life as it already exists not
Understood better about needing
The lucky stone wasn't finished
I loved the printed page
The vision itself may move in and out
Whose eye is smitten by the crucial thing
People give pain
Soberer than we
Learning stamps you
During the big flu
By boring her eyes through me
Scissored out in the shapes of the sun
Setting out in this world
He didn't hurry you off
Disappointing that books are written by persons
It was taken entirely for granted
In those days the dark was dark
I have always been shy
I don't remember that any secrets were revealed
Grown up in religious households in our own
Life in a crowd
Dramatically working up to
The only man teacher in the college
My little red Royal portable
A delicate dagger into Mademoiselle's left side
Since this was a weekday morning
I was truly in its grip
I never wrote another such story
Greater than situation is implication
As the New York train pulled
Part-time or temporary jobs

Those were the last years
They pressed at the pomegranate stains
Her fingers slid down
This is a white dance
Trembling over her tall body
Anyone could have had that

LITTLE CARBON BOOK

I would be fixing a ground
A viewer has no place here
Illumination is a controller
Should not be tampered with
To bungle a good idea
The editor has written me
De-emphasize discovery in mathematics
The case is often made
One begins to realize
The idea is read about rather than looked at
The word is a portable sign
The mysterious being known as God
A zero word
World as a whole and museums business
Executives corporate public relations officers
Pictures quoted in pictures
We do everything directly
Or even spell to the hospital chief
Children are the cruelest of all
I want to recall what I always knew
I want to eroticize time
Make something which lives
Articulate something
The function I am engaged in
That's his business it's not up to me
The art of others better than his own
He makes slick art

PURPLE VINYL

The chair tipped and the table tipped. The dim light lit a statement that was atmospherically contemporary. Within herself she held her body poised like a sensitive microphone, a chip. I needed a reason or person to spend a night in your room. I might put a knee on your couch the way a mountaineer notices the light climbing the rock face far above but doesn't stop and wonder, only withdraws a crampon and moves up. The number on the bubble indicating voicemails silently ticked a few higher. This girl on the train has a dancer's body and the tough glance of a martinet. She wears too-tight sweats below a razor-flat lip. If she wanted a kiss I wouldn't say no. Some people are born into money, others articulate misery or just yawn. For weeks I didn't feel hunger until just after dinner. I buzzed her in. The hallway is green, the air is green, I put on Can, you have the green beans album. Later I'm on the L Train again. The person with whom I came to the opening and then I noticed a man with a mullet, not the ironic kind, a studious Teutonic man you can't help laugh at behind his back, but not at the mullet, it's not funny enough in context, I think he's German, he passes by, passes the time, with a high stuck laugh. It could be a cough, but is a laugh after all. You're so weak, you say, since you talk to yourself in the second person. You think he's laughing at you. Because everything is a comedown to him, you conjecture, sarcasm is his lifeblood, though he wouldn't say "lifeblood," he would never put it that way, it's too sincere, which is unbearable hyperbole. Whether he laughs at you or at another person or thing is all the same. He is a dispenser of high stuck laughter, an atomizer just spraying the air around him with chortle, an atomizer from Bavaria in pencil shorts. You are not there to see the Bavarian but the painting of an artist you know in Vancouver. It is a joke just for the two of you, every month or so, to say "I only know you by your art anymore" or "I just want to kiss your installation" or "Your catalogue said hello for you." Only you don't send any art to Vancouver. In the small office off the bathroom a woman is spreadeagled on the floor as if post 'total knockout,' but then you can't see her head which is stuck up the waist of a fussy, delicate, hollow resin plinth stuck with LEDs, unplugged. Some remark involving the word 'naughty' or as deliberately corny as ‘things are looking up,’ but she never knows I am there, or ignores me with breathtaking sangfroid. Late that night it was really almost morning I tripped and fell. I am still getting used to the new place and, look, my toe tipped into a largish hole in the flooring. When I got my balance I got down on my knees. I thought I heard very far away down that hole some dance music, I guess I could say “techno,” and the smell of an artificial smoke machine, an odor like when your purple vinyl jacket got caught in the escalator at the Museum of Modern Art. Then there was real smoke too and with that tangy plastic smell and we were both pulling at your jacket just hard as all hell, laughing.

MOLLY RINGWALD

I could have added them to bump
the convo up they say Molly
scrunch a sock in pocket
you were the one to love mute
odorous unquiet remembrance
to fall over anything steel wool
kiss toe line under Jesus come on
in pieces of rope belt not to be
seen out of all your friends apart
at keg won't happen near
you fell over today Monday
plucked out oyster shell for shiv
you would have swung harder
if knowing the prize is fixed
packages at reception dinner late
dirty dank face in blue plate
and noticed hair round nipples
his swank out of place ass
we woke in suburban New
Jersey what is New Jersey to
an oblique murmur as they say
passive hurtful postage franks
drones under two types of sodium
blueprints line the trip before and
maps everywhere made of violence
you say I wish you wouldn't
take your advice but it is all
I have to loan you theories stories
you could take some up and apart
a brainstorm system cooling
a reflex nod toward coming night
behind the hills behind us buildings
we put chests together meaning off
I want to be gone there again
a moment of togetherness

WHITE ON WHITE

Don't you know I like
you like I put you on hold
again heavy as a jungle gym
constantly repainted weigh
many moments I don't press
inward or engage strangers
white on white the smokers' shed
at school he stood outside
looking ideal it was his fingers
a passing reaction you tracking him
you bore through the rest
then to stymie a liquid notion
of hell as a burning ocean
why don't you eat more I said
only twice silently but with my eyes
because it is by putting things inside
bigger firmer looser flush
with the ground put things in
the girl she did invent a black
hand inflated a rubber sock
to trail its kite tail resonant
across roof tiles pink and beige
no more plans for island
I prefer to take your tongue tip
for now for later fall asleep
never wake except to another
straight face to midtown facework
good grief tower floors resonate
spicier television kids dream of
transparency and static chew
and when hurt say God Jesus God
free the worst of us creep here
now for a limited time ripe
with noises cold velvet curtains
nuanced views on Europe

looking daggers at the kid's show
folded over the desk like a broken
veteran a cutthroat teenage
hand bare of rings finger a mark
below dark stares unchecked

CATCH PLAY

missing missing one at speed one
you use done behaviors right drizzle
sinister conversations startle up dust
stab bleary sob public blush display
so real your halter me sudden thighs
and inside of silk arms slide to grip
my laugh to you baby baby soft slow
dried blue forgotten negatives crackle
across pocket glass to spy fresh wines
my spaz be about us squirt play catch
flutes lemon love loss leader sell that meat
by Friday social here pose teenage pathos
jerk flares half your mouth slips down get
saddle gripped hard like swing chain letters
down to den beanbag phone out so it cracks
drag each and all wall-to-wall rug burned kids
pick nits and quarters from shag Buddha
elect the cutthroat deadpan rep meaner
baby's first word processor delete press
sodden fingers grope round shower nozzle
mimic unknown tones to drop zipper
certain others offer things out of reach
the sun now wanes or lifts off leafy ledge
cups in shadow sills cool and mold up
these fluids she refuses tell nothing new
for boys as good as find it all keep mum
cover inkier my passed out pasty
you leave from French windows in fall
coldish palm stained with dangerous tea
grading papers polishing tiles make out
small cares blunted legs less numb now
what afternoon is this vanilla wafers flavors
close eyes faster overhead branches creak

SAME TIME

off seed your big cloud nine number
wet nights yours too heated limber you
as students twist parts from hidden pants
headlines bruise life studies to be clipped also torn
such delay say I have not been unsteady much
this month dug back out piled platonic ills
mirrors see you help yourself be less favored
for lassies a plenty maybe when are you ready
to cup with open under-lip such soil as hits
when brittle little breast tips wave fetch in gloaming
watch more matured peers modulate scenery with mirage
and me my cock and you more unsure whom to pity
house kid months thrusting icepick to flat of land
family only held your young brow down hurting
so you can tell cubicle meat today from cubicle lock
green blonde hair messy fucking hot just now
a whiff of male piss about your earlobes
I don't know I guess I haven't earned anything
won't you stick to me this time dear fellow my lay
your flattish roving tits with little hairs in sprig by anus
I don't know feed the children from fingering aimlessly
your inelegant thighs seated upright as if for landing
you direct me slow my shove place my mouth near waist
nose me toward riverbed under sky hood I could die
could balance a coin on your thoughtful swallowing
bring salt that must spread through your bluer blood
your pulses your pants so soft stained of reasons of duties
stems making shadows cross each other in near shallows
when we brush blue fruit and come to and see stars arise

HURT THE STREAM

Impossible the same. To stumble rain come cover of the same substance. As in an Italian town to lean. A tuning fork of no sound. All scraps of material similar. Still some painted. To amplify that which you cannot not attend, cannot not process. From the cheap seats a wave at this being scattered activity. A scattering as of chaff. Look at my cheek and you would, you are the girls. Including boys and young men and men. Many men would surprise. Dropping them, these shapes, like knives to gouge at obtuse angles the perturbed lap of water. It doesn't hurt. You can't hurt it. Elements of unfeeling. Push down on the grain at hand, under palm. As if to flick a soundless chord, untune sediment, mock up a story. Make a mush of spray, a milk drop shot fast and still, crowning, beaded at your tips, unseen dust where your other wet dust just drizzled. Impossible to stumble again. To be underfoot. To loaf toward rocks like loaves. Just another anthem under breath, a ballad. Come over come across I have spray my sweet one. A leaning pillar of no community of learning. A coin lost or forgotten, a signature stumble. If they did not see the tower. Defunct surveillance. To flick a splatter pattern. Town sphincter rise up to mourn the dead shot dead. The new bridge out of scale, hung with too many devices. A synthesized disturbance made synthetic, made artificial, made sweetener. Unused blocks watch motionless around them stream suds. A seam in the land in which to stumble again, but not that. Look and you would. Look, that is. A monument of light labor, all glancing so that no four eyes can meet in this clearing. We are all here because we are not all there. The water stepping from above itself always across and down, across and down, like some loon. Bridge lamps on timer blink up. I think I did it wrong, wet as I am to the tip of my crown. I will stop calling. Just talk to me. Give me a word, words to sound off against. Impossible to not once to not drop one on one's leg, one's foot. So the girl can only form an impression from a particular viewpoint, and boys and the young men and men. Minor humorist would say impossible is the same. To squeeze back toward a kind of neuter act as found at the outset of tales. Impossible not to do it wrong. Not to step into. Not the same. Could take, could make, and why other boredoms, purple-faced leashes, purple-faced clouds. Low groans where feet like knives cut or scissor down. You can get across on foot. To stumble of the same substance some ninety percent impossible. So it's true. The ones that looked are gone.

NOTHING TO WATCH BUT THE ROAD

love plants cold kicks
such sweepings
muster precocious forces
mists about potted
rooftop trees you see
snot on wall by can
but can I love to look
plants she said
roots insensate tangle
rings turn you clear
shaves can't erase
eating nothing smoggy
skies Camels mints
status meaning no
clearer come likes
warning buzz promotes
a show of nerves
of ciphers coolly move
things us included like
coffee sells mugs mugs buy
when worser stories
go on periodically
grip home tools
balding innocence buds
soft surgeon palm
not your defter fingers
plinths metal swag
know you have feelings
because thus stab at gut
as if from outside
your own emotions
missiles fall tugging
parachutes crinkly cash
Canadian whiskey nylons
wire transfers going

down on a quarter
under Oldsmobile
your spine stiff your thoughts
kiddo knew baby honey
to blueprint alone time
during world war infinity
further into clocked heart
prick final flag pant
you reach inside and pull
your string
and everyone
is out to
get you mother fuck-
er

AMERICAN TERRORIST

I am what I thank you for this killing
you saved me you said you couldn't pay
heat in cafés clipped thread of story um
numbers in your note application a tune
a flame yet to be a divot of orange wick
how do you wash shirts for smoke clings
thinking this is okay recorded after all
black sidewalk gum won't be peeled
letting trains roll that you don't need
a soloist leaning as if to get back in it too
I used to steal from myself and forget why
be indignant I was robbed traveler
every dollar tripe soup hashish coffee
the sun kneeling on far horizon water
getting up after a drunk Oxy stumble
I thought we would fuck again another
shoebox empty accused the broom boy
me they found missing camera cuts
I felt I was striking after a lifted siege
a clatter of cups at the nearer table at back
I thought we would have sex more again
Billy Joel blamed the fire on not we but
when you get steamed you have ways
honey I salute tomorrow for longer out
sick I check my watch it's again at head

THIS IS FOR YOU

To sever alive the limb
he was a tree
day withered
unseasonable heat felt
a heavy rabbit cloth
upon the lips the visitor
went coy a daytime moon
work from home
always from home
chip of daytime moon
mirror the mantelpiece
just for show purpose
take off at door
I am confident hardwood
paper leaves
such writ as Kant changed
the point is not to get the statement
the random number generator
for fun must not as such work
but for a smile of recognition
not fooling anyone
they all would have died
they would have just died
eyes closed like a doll's

PROFESSOR MARVEL

each marble tells certain stories I have
while something else is cooking the books
so in between you try frying me around sleep
my heart still going from that treadmill
at once in several stay with me I'll say
December colander clear ears you pushy
loops back though war is never declared
one long half hour mute why did you step
back and stones in air dust mineral particles
some white felon bunkered knowing warming
I feel differently now you have piqued me
we are just here to make bigger posters
now a community center poor loans
plinths for sitting cushions stitched
neat from coffee sacks march backwards
into a time capsule different holds boys
we have identified who really have girls have
identified themselves girls of every skin tone
why do you call me international ghost
lost cane speedy gone salads pecans *aperçus*
pecans apricots inkwells again letters
passages about maps the idea of calligraphy
a dusty wall with brown black smudges
get into your body and you stay there till death
but in Sausalito a rolling stone inkwell
even when planted they are readily surprised
to romp in romper rooms swallow me number
my body made for shaded room at back
green I came here from sacked territories
and you in vacuum silo full of artifacts only
obscured by alps by protagonists fired by
an arc of moving vision aimed at all ears
three hundred and sixty marathon runners
begin running in every direction at once

THURSDAY I FORGET HER NAME

we have granted you entry
whom you address later months
attempts windy mostly male dross
awake you let you click unlike
yonder wall of clouds cloaking
these our few blocks doors all lock
I am flirting subtle so it's lost on me
face to face I am Chris for today
to learn to heal to screw to fight
more wisdom teething frozen cash
wake up somewhere sunny
bundled morning half of afternoon
door slammed open unhinged bald
for your own good one knows catch
you redolent of midnight oil
final spatula in your fist no threat
we have granted you entry
floors humming with grey water
pipes in walls rushing receipts
confinement good for one haptic
trip on clods strange ways reverse
droning on on late diaries cards
we have granted you entry
to times else left what skips in place
to talk just say so you learn too fast
to heal to screw to chorale new fights
not to kill up in here but tap foot
exact in time me drunken drummer
lovely woman child man infant tears
it is a sunrise sunset eye roll daub
lets us sleep again as one tap drips loud
to lay again wet cold carpet flat
had I been alone would had
gone out for good having chosen
never to agree again for her

HOMEGROWN CELL

I know little about the attacks of this year
a long train delay heart splits my aspirin
I'm going to hell having drunk each ink
without leaning forward or back
opening my mouth I not quite bite
thus with fork return to park litter
weather allowing warmer invites
temporary crystals crushed in her belly
pale brandy hallway lamps smell of her
stays us all the same who stray on
put in harness flatten empties fast a bit
to scan rooms just two steps of eye
the way a knight is meant to move in chess
mystery over your shoulder device at waist
honey of vinyl in room you are stuck in
amber loans love savings beats subsonic
I need Jesus to stray back into time
I need a hunt to color my cheek
a small clean window to reflect in swift
anger glowing there too swings cat jazz
I assign no person brush these strings
take identifying spray for smashed glass
if I see some there you were vandal
of water afire on Mars new screensavers
I say astonish stay on I know this prayer nook
stay on this carousel stay you flaming resident
crash into my pocket one more time still

TAPE HISS

If I made you a tape, I know what song I'd put on, I'm not telling. Press play. Press record. Put keys down together. Hard so it clicks, holds. For a second everything listens, all pulling further things inside, not the ambient air but particulates hanging in among the eyehooks of atmosphere in flux. Dusts, resonances of dumb things, the kitchen sink, plaster, furniture, cats, a cat's name shouted, the jacket that kid left, broken hearts, violins. I could take a record company factory issue commercial compact cassette, let it be born to run, beige plastic and black type, thumb sticky Scotch strips to seal erase-protection tabs. Sometimes you might take a small brush of office product and smudge sticky reeking goop over identifiers. Cake on Wite-Out let the shell dry over a weekend maybe get you high. Presidents' Day. Memorial Day. Turkey day. Here is a sticky, smelly snowball she can hear. A botched artificial egg he can waggle at roommates. Even gob-caked it will fit a special person's yellow Walkman, his boom-box, her car's dashboard slot. It turns better after toothpicking. Start making lists, keep melodies in mind, forget some parts, misremember others. How it starts off, song three, first song on the Side B, the last tune that will get cut abrupt, probably edited. There is nothing to not erase. Much too much nothing. All there is. Tapes you erase as you go, always, because this is how new wonder works: capture, replay, decay, tangle, computer monitor disaster. Shake and see. Etch A Sketch of noise. First thing you can write music on then write music over former songs write it with music again wipe all when putting down your own words spoken. A blackboard big as a marquee, high and heavy as planes afar descending. A thin orange crayon yards long, a sponge that dampens above roofs, the squeak of hinge or mouse. Everything now a mistake, just a take, a scratched take, okay, this is take three. An act of theft a piracy outlaw you share crimes. Property promotional. So you show another what you have stolen and this bravery breeds intimacy. Another economy when you can exploit scarcity or getting the stuff in advance. You have to choose. Always you could have chosen other moments, other seconds, other spaces, other sounds, other songs, other stations, other words, other friends, other lovers, other orders, other passive intentions. You missed out, you know it. You in fact just are this missing, sodden archive of unlogged roads traveled. Where were you two weeks ago this past Friday. Who saw you. What was spoken. Hit record, though, you may as well turn your back away. You have to turn your back to look forward to what you haven't heard, to crouch toward that. What surrounds like a weak particulate dust shower appears more fully upon letting go, letting the electricity flow. Black Steel in the Hour of Chaos. While My Guitar. Fuck and Run. Stuck Inside of Memphis. The tapes you brought with you and those they furnished you with. You put them near some fruits or rank vegetables, they grow molds, whine, crackle and break. Atomic. Why Can't I Touch It. Computer speakers, dashboard sun, the rubberized pad clerks slide items on. What does it do. Where does it go. Such plastic trash could outlast roaches. Read it in a magazine you borrow. Who will be there to touch it. An artificial exemplar, analogue soul, brittle bones stiff at rest, at peace if you say so. Making anything means erasing, clear cutting, even if only the high clean hiss of a blank Maxell freshly unwrapped. Talk into the built-in and you can wipe, replace a piece of song with what you said just then that afternoon. Private jokers. Everything you could ever say deletes all that else could have been heard, now never will. Was she waiting to be polite or waiting for a thing you have. Was he listening for a moment to start something or just being kind. Destroying ruins to dig them up further. Flushed silence erasing words you could have asked. Guess how much is left on this side. Could you fit one more tune, may it be best and shortest, or put on a long one so they'll know you knew it'd get cut off and what of it. Oh the ragman draws circles up and down the block no blind spots in the leopard's eyes losing the star without the sky when I go to Baltimore need no carpet on my floor you know man when I was a young man in high school in the day we sweat it out on the streets of a runaway American dream be on my side I'll be on your side baby well you greet the tokens and stamps underneath the fake oil-burning lamps when I heard the knock on the door I couldn't catch my breath hey little girl I wanna be she's not a girl who misses much I'm coming out of my cage well I'm craving for a cigarette hey give me a light people cry people die for you people kill people will for you I see you you see me watch you blowing the lines I'm in love with my girl she is away instead of carving up the wall why don't you open up with talk.

WILD BUNNY PIE

Lift it off the gearshift look back
at small bags packed with weight
under steel lid pollen eddies
past quarry you could get tickets to dive
down cold would pop you back out and up
sour apples your blonde green hair
drying in a paste at crown of neck
rusted legs of kitchen chairs roadside
moon up not far from the sun your hairy arm
feet out the window pushed air
through sneaker grommets fingers spread
to have been taller by graduation
chin thrust to chest the bus you would not
ever tell her what you knew so little
that could be phrased bleeding bruise
inside baseball but enough
to stand up at a desk and walk out
through frothy edges of movement circles
riding mower over vacation home lawns
energetic in the guest house or bar roof
finally a chill when sunrise pinks flat clouds
angry like a crying child who forgot why
the sum taken from the larger sum
left on its own remains intact to the cent
a pill sours your tongue you shut the phone
considering inviting into a sublet room
makings to eat and sleep late the boss
hardly heard of all things a telegram
how to find out if a death means travel
calculate the miles and days till ropes are taut
faces hardening at the slight misplaced grin
wallet thick with receipts and stubs smells cut
he had to get home eventually good manners
at any time of night you could wake him
he didn't want to party with you though he ate

wiped fried skin bits into a cone of wax paper
forgot wallet there the pine arm sure
any excuse she arose made hot water
razor in cup holder banana on the dash
cruise control to Alabama
recite drama mind of boy boy boy O

KNOW YOUR NAME

the safe place the skyline
behind the window
above the wall
it was a witless a witless that weekend
her fear in cabs her fear of new persons
a witless bar crawl
they were the masters
their lobbies empty
I told her for years I'd had that green comforter
a witless disregard of duty that we laughed
even what she might choose for me
take all the plastic from a city
it could hold
unwrap a disposable toothbrush while watched
a new night
docile I slept five times on the broken box bed
the pain was incredible but the pills
dancing in the day room with Sarah
before the apartment door kissing Lisa
the owners of a store outed her
for a rube or con or worse
a personal shopper
Lisa's adventure in July glare
blent into LCD coming up on other girls' laps
my head there or never to be
egging each other on
in all seriousness fart jokes or worse
blasting purity the venomed politesse fooled all but us
hours constructing a Midwestern propriety
of dress the filth she'd address only to me
to stand on the platform at Bergen
more like a shard than any other
to be drunken starting in the afternoon
at hand always fresh lemon slices
squinting into feathers rising above down pillows

too perfect naked from each distance of view
it happened it is time to wait
showing me life is artificial and kills all imagining
fleshed shaped from inside on a wheel
the flag drooping in heat
veterans calling after coins
through the air conditioner
the buildings exhaling the mind poisons
and on the roof of Bellevue West graffiti
heartbreakingly accepting of the probable
don't come back to see us now
hope I never see you again
a basketball clips my ankle
in the corner where the sun
the Chrysler Christ I took a wafer once
all the Christian Dylan I sang in CPEP
an inmate self-castrated
on the rolling bed before mine
having found a safety razor
peeled it open he sprayed blood
my first thought was to get out of the spray
they rolled him on his rolling bed away
just remember that bed
and think of the bed before that
and the one before that
and so remembering bed by bed
you can think of all the walls
all the horizons
all the women and men and children
who sheltered you
where you were
you are a child hardly before you forget
know your name
remember your name
your name is

WE MAY BE FREE

I feel danger door can't see where
one meaning many I do have trust
as mercury lines a hothouse petal
until for a moment she's gone then so
smart for her own good finds paths
from clearings where ideas smudged
are ugly potent catalysts to focus formations
I am glad to talk about anything blank
like myself being a torchbearer trying
to point but only can gesture swaths of light
meant on foam-rubber beds heels shucked
wherever she walked under windows dark
open to various infestations never animal
touch of third rail red blush on her cheek
today my tongue gets flavor of data loss
the future a sack of inert gas no one will know
to wait on more snow slush permission
I see her on a slab on a cot in a war
she will make it through she thrums anyway
doesn't allow we may be free each to each
to slur disappointed phrases anxious ten
I don't know minutes something happened
and the ball was out of air slapped a sill
came under sneakers now squeaks a block off
games of patience alluded to in her nod
to a third stranger a word for returning keys
those hers and it wasn't like what I wanted
face down on a stranger's couch close too
taking it taking it never to tie a bow
a word of concern not for all the others
a line under small fires have to burn down
to no paper no notebook no jacket no kiss
nothing for louder spaces but powder traces
the star she put in my throat like gum back up
can't swallow two fingers split why it must

be that memory something middle outlines
I don't know something happened a pause
I wrote this all before half knowing the end
among hatches in the evening howling steel
girders in air grievance frog mouse swallow cat
a purple onion moldering classic woodcut
shelved so she took over for a spell no favors
so you get down you public male identity got
at staircase top papered skylight attempts a tear
pull your finger out pop makes seam lower pop
jetliner on ordered dark trajectory takes me not
how will I know you landed amid frost and plans
the hands in your purse electric anyway alive
turn it it chimes a sigh anxiety rip is my fault made
now angle of incidence slower now slow now over
so I don't have much to speak of never did
have put a bed straight could you put me down
first thought best thought class there no teacher
in Tennessee I have not made it far knowing a spear
could grow through skin through Tibet Mexico
witnesses from my hat bill sneaker toe you can take
fighting how possession wipes glasses with a rind
the one mud path we see protesters or scientists say
null and if I posed with one hand on brow
looking down chasms hidden behind door
there in surround I have said I love you
with a wound I can't see I can't see going solo
to a further edge perhaps last square in sad story
the heat in my quiver probably part cruel fire

SO MANY FORTRESSES

in memory of Eric Garner

People need to give me love. You're coming
to, you're coming too, peg up no
side, sunny vertical a group outside
light poles I guess I want to
be myself, be someone new
steady in the need of prayer
the melody starts
immediately, don't get stuck, please,
it's louder.

Seems 1968, 1968, nodding to what you feel
is flowing inside. Don't get stuck please.
Not my brother, it's me it needs
to, it needs to be to
lint, knit, back black shirt.

Speckle chrome Sony hard head most
people focus on Watts
the person who is thinking about gears,
stands, smile walks
friar to hair girl, churl, the black nub.

Why falsetto ghetto key people need to give
me love light poles, standing
in the need of prayer
key of C, two one-way mirror her
band, not my mother not
my father but it's me, shhh.

Lord insulted, bah bah bah sssshh.

A simple person, some things
take effect
on me that I couldn't understand. It's not art.

This is a stick-up, a stick, stainless steel.

Remedial crown, left
side of the mirror, four hundred, forty thousand, one
thousand listen to herself. People need to get me, wave
them back, the waves black.

It seemed like it was a battle, thick glass, but it's me
O Lord, it's me
that melody, shirts fur ball do no see
my interior brrrrring brrrrring brrrring bringing.

Simple person some things take
effect on me that I could not
understand it's not
art you can overdub them.

Nobody cares what I'm saying.

Can you try with what you're singing? Don't
get stuck, please.

The music is not different, the only thing that is
different is the lyrics. Marine
Corps, I can't get next to you, this is
a stick-up. The windows, Windex,
it's not art, you could overdub them.

Stainless steel, medical crown a peaceful other
menus the receiver what do those
people this is a stick-up stainless
steel medical crown left side of the mirror.

Listen to herself.

It seemed like it was a battle they had
to clean out the building. Unlawful assembly started
beating ass again we can't
use the gun we pick
it up like '45 you gonna use the rifle
regardless of what often young
people I want to judge from
my experience standing in the need of prayer.

I used to watch television as a boy
I used to watch I do not see my interior
the outside needs to be you
come on, family Marine Corps check out, deer buff
insulted Indians, this is a stick-up.
Simple person some
things take effect on me effort
I couldn't understand it's not art
you can overdub them nobody cares what I'm saying.

Don't get stuck please.

Can we try with your singing? The music
is not different, the only thing that is
different is the lyrics,
smash the windows, I cry,
baaah baaah buh buh baaah baaah.

Needs to be you write the different words
is making art, tangle of syntax, can you try with
your singing can you try
with your seeing singing, nodding to
what you feel is flowing inside what
do these people want?

All I can see seems louder it is 1958, '68, 19-flat, flat,
C's are written in reverse triptych two-plet we all can't think
properly seems like I couldn't come
back to myself back then, left
different music, hell Victoria write
the different words malign, liner, I don't know,
it's too busy, it doesn't settle
like a line in a groove could overdub it.
Are you kidding?

All I could see was white men their use
of guns on the Indian.

It needs to be you, too, thing that was the only
way that you could see. Thing that needs
to be accomplished the way you can say it
with her eyes that melody starts
immediately, irremediably, immediately,
a word: patience, patience not me, not to hide
impatience grip ball mike stand heels in
the Marine Corps sure is flat
flat flat why falsetto ghetto troll
bowtie the black
nub people need to give me love.

You're coming to,
you're coming to.

The police were surrounding the Panthers's
office, the Panthers, the Panthers, the Panthers's office, one
of the sisters, Panthers, that was, Panthers out there Angela
Davis she got beat that night.
I guess I want to be myself, be someone new
standing in the need of prayer like polis not my
mother not my father, but it's me.
O Lord two one-way mirror her.

And see and see fancy fancy I have to adjust the mike-
stand grip ball one
brother's heels is louder, boots, boost what do
these people boost nodding too
what you feel is flowing inside to myself it
needs to be that is the only way I could see
that father, that brother it's me, not my
brother, not my father, all
I would see is white men, use of gun
on television on Indian, they was
shooting the only way I could
see that things would gear
stands, gear, gear, gear smile walks.

Friar through hair churl, churl bow
tie the black nub, you're coming to, you're coming
too, they were scared, that's
why I believe violence worked there.

They were scared, that's why. I believe
violence worked there. They were
scared, that's why. I believe violence
worked there. Think about gears think about gear
Apple chrome Sony chrome.

Knit back black shirt the person most people focus on
Watts they were scared that's why
I believe violence worked there. Smile Watts fingers
through hair churl bow tie the black tie egg cup no
side sunny side weekend a group outside
weekend a group outside. What will you do weekend
a group outside. Top lip, triptych where can't I
think purposefully seems like could
not come back to myself lately left different
music to hell Victoria, left hell Victoria.

That's the only way they could
see it, they were scared. I believe violence worked there, why
falsetto you're coming too, you're coming to, people need
to give me love the black nub bowtie churl through hair
smile walks friar fingers in groove
through hair there in different grooves the words
maligned can you try it?

It is not the music. Can you try with your singing,
are you kidding?
T-shirt open there is no guitar there
is no guitar I think this guy in here is gone
comprehend them ships
up commanding captain in Alaska
I am playing manicure phone poles are light
poles black balloon loops
the unfocused posters lowers so blue
black banana in ear palette different words
for the second under smoke, smock, the windows under
guitar changes nobody cares
what I'm saying. Read L. A. City Ambulance. Read
L. A. City Ambulance there is
no guitar.

Regardless of what, o yeah, he's like Malcolm
X, I wanted to say, caution, he's
like Teddy Gibson, whatever that is.

There is no guitar.

They made him an admirable. They made him an admiral.
No laughter. Bad dynamics, this is work, don't fuck up
on off-key, a revolutionary, bad man baton baton
fellowship yes I was net, shirt, little house, *haus*, the tiny
piano makes the call sell ring can he sing
what brand of egg read that hmm, I did

crunch for you, they're coming true
gyro zero star reverse center
people need to give me love. To help me, the Panther
office out the building I've seen
bullets I guess we've just got on
have to wait three black shadow doors, two
black shadow doors, two black shadow doors what
does she know, nodding in time, the white
horizontal leaves falling trapped holds
the stiff black framed typical rod
nullifies multiplies her digital past
in color when we are the same people some
people it seems like it was a battle nobody cares what
I'm saying, nor earth nor sky.

They were scared, that's why I believe violence
worked there. Why falsetto, you're coming too.
People need to give her love, people
need to give me love
one of the sisters, not
my brother, not my father, it's me. Don't get
stuck please, one brother, he's in the Marine Corps all
I would see what do these
people want, nodding to each other
it's louder.

1968 it's 2014, where I can't think
properly seems like I wouldn't come
back right then, left different
music like I don't know, it's too lousy, it doesn't settle, kissing
the ball tangle of guitar, could overdub it
in a groove are you kidding? Freddy Gibson?

Whatever that sure is flat flat C's written in reverse. They were scared,
that's why I believe violence worked there. Thinking about gears,
stands, smiles walks fingers through hair

churl bowtie the black nub people need to give
me love. Nobody cares what I'm saying. Eggs no side sunny, textual
textual on a weekend in a group outside right. Band brand brandy.
I guess I want to be someone, be myself, new.

Standing in the need of prayer. People need to give me love.
Why falsetto, you're coming to, they were scared
that's why I believe violence worked there. Thinking about gears
stands speckle chrome thinking about it's louder all eye
brothers eye melody immediately accomplish could see
needs be hell the different words making tangle guitar
can you try? I don't know it's too lousy seems
like I couldn't where I can't think, sure, flat, flat triptych no side
sunny eggs white poles see huh. Standing in the need of prayer,
she got beat that Angela. I guess I want to be someone new.
Be and brandy brand band bee and they were scared
that's why I believe violence worked there. Knit back, black shirt
thinking back gears stance walks
fingers through hair churl churl churl most
people focus on Watts. The person who all I would see was a white man
his use of a gun on an Indian on television.

It needs to be you!

Not my brother, not my father, it's me, don't get stuck please.

I have to adjust the mike-stand, O it's me O Lord, band.
That melody starts thick glass I used to watch
television a lot. Do not see my interior fur ball.
The outside is so c'mon needs to
be you, family, Marine Corps I can't get next to you.

This is a stick-up.

O I see I side smashed a window
simple person some things take effect on me,

it's not art, the music is not different the only thing that's different
is the lyrics, you can overdub them nobody
cares what I'm saying can you try can we try with singing? Don't
get stuck, please.

A revolution, peaceful.

Other means of recurrence. What do these people this is
a stick-up. Stainless steel, medical crown, left side
of the mirror ten thousand, twenty thousand, 2014.

Listen to herself, people need to get me. Wave them
black it seemed like it was a battle. Filmed
black, they helped clean up the building. A man
unlawful assembly, they started beating ass again, I mean
man unlawful assembly, they started
beating ass again a man, unlawful assembly, they started beating
ass again, film black ten thousand, forty thousand,
a revolution peaceful other means
if recent buildings falling I used to watch television a lot,
do not see my interior, fur ball the outside is so
c'mon common needs to be you I
can't get next to you not my father not
my brother common the building's fallen, the people fallen, you
can overdub them nobody cares what I'm saying,
can we try with you singing? Can we be friends on facebook?

Simple person?

Sure is flat, flat, c's are written in reverse tuck
with triptych, but I can't think purposefully I can't think
in terms of practice. All I could see
was white men use of gun to conquer Indians
on television it needs to be you.

That was the only way I could see that things
could be accomplished black men shirt on black

speckled chrome they were scared, that's why
I believe violence worked there. They were scared,
that's why I believe violence worked there. They were scared, that's why
I believe violence worked there. They
were scared, that's why I believe violence
worked there. Why falsetto? You're coming to, you're coming too.
Green light green light nobody cares
what I'm saying eggs sunny side up
people need to give me love.

ACKNOWLEDGEMENTS

Earlier versions of these poems appeared in *The American Poetry Review*, *Circus Book*, *Denver Quarterly*, *New American Writing*, *Pittsburgh Poetry Review*, *Prelude*, *Red Savina Review*, *VOLT*, and *White Wall Review*.

"Fresh Stubble Air" was commissioned for painter Bettina Marx's exhibition "Remodeling," and first published in Melissa Canbaz, Jürgen Dehm, Chris Hosea, *Bettina Marx: Remodeling*. Münster, Germany: Verlag Kettler, 2014.

"Tape Hiss" was commissioned for painter Terence Hannum's exhibition "Impedence," and first published in *Terence Hannum: Impedence*. Baltimore, Maryland: Stevenson University Art Gallery, 2015.

"Hurt the Stream" was commissioned by sculptor Charlie Schneider for his forthcoming catalogue, *Charlie Schneider: Cinderblock Project*.

I thank the editors, curators, and artists.

For fellowship residencies that helped in the making of these poems, I am grateful to Omi International Arts Center and The Vermont Studio Center.

Thank you: John Ashbery, Rob Crawford and Stu Watson, Kim Bennett, Peter Gizzi, Myles Paige, Mel Prest, Will Georgantas, Joe Fletcher, Jeff Goldberg, Douglas Piccinnini, Ariana Reines, Rachelle Rahme—and especially Lillian Tong.

ABOUT THE AUTHOR

Chris Hosea was born in Princeton, New Jersey. He is also the author of *Put Your Hands In* (LSU Press, 2014), which was selected by John Ashbery for the Walt Whitman Award from the Academy of American Poets. He lives in Brooklyn, New York.